Red

James McInerney

Also by James McInerney:

In Between the Lines

Bloom

The bit before the poems.

This book is dedicated to all
the people on this planet that
remain forgotten and yet still
carry on regardless, with hope
in their hearts.
You are the true heroes.

This entire book was hand typed on my
Scheidegger Princess-Matic typewriter
using A4, one hundred and thirty GSM,
high quality white cartridge paper.

I am officially a Poet!!
I have been writing since '98 and
I decided it was about time, three
books and over 350 poems later,
to mark the occasion with a tattoo.
A thousand thanks to Malcolm Buswell,
an amazing Tattoo Artist.
Check out Malcolm on Instagram
@malcybabes17

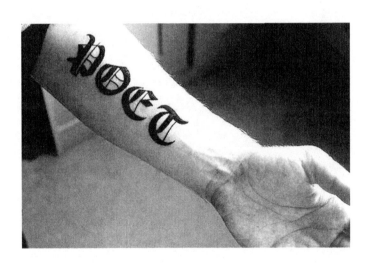

'RED'

I want you

Passing cars

Final embrace

When I leave

Gone

Masterpiece

Believe in better

Ripcord

Cry

Empty vessel

Home

Real love

I am fire

Glass

She often dreams

The power of the sky

The right kind of balance

She

Change

Equal measures

Wild flower

Static

Moments

You

Sunshine and rain

A heart full of love
Beautiful
Straight lines
Bridges
Wings
Oxygen
Papercuts
Tragic things
Fire and rain
Flowers
All the things
Ghost
Cold bones
The girl in the mirror
All the lights
A light that burns bright
Human kindness
I am more
Same sky
Let it be
You and I
As he stood before her
My biggest mistake
I love you
Target practice

Taller than trees

Beauty

Storm chaser

Collide

Sunshine

Music

Forever love

Avenues and alleyways

Angels and monsters

Alone

I am in love with the sea

Writing to remember

I am my own island

Hide and seek

The longest pause

My star

Perfectly aligned

In every possible moment

Beneath the sky

Jacket

The right side of bad

I came back

My moon

Not me, not I

Fortress

Heavy heart

Learning to fly

A flame

Time

Eternal

An angel

Everywhere I go

Stones

Flames

Bleeding heart

Stars

A darkened room

Work of art

I found myself in you

Fingertips

I became fire

Me and you

Sorrow

Walls

"Red is how you make me feel,
the kind of red that does
not heal that easily."

- James McInerney.

A massive thanks to all the lovely people
that have supported me via my Patreon
account during the writing of this book;
your support means so much to me.

Patrons:

Ariel Thomae
Instagram : @a_thomae23

Dayanara Hurn
Instagram : @dayanarahurn

Sally Anne Beere

Sarah Elliott
Instagram : @sazlou1985

https://www.patreon.com/jamesmcinerney

Pause for thought.

Thank you for buying me, however, do not read
me all at once; read me only when you need me.
I am not meant to be read in one sitting,
it would be too much, too overwhelming and it
wouldn't make sense. I am a book of poems
and each poem has a different story to tell,
they are not meant to co-exist as though they
were a continuous story.
Keep me on a shelf, live your life, let the
dust settle and when life lets you down or
becomes confusing, which at some point it will,
find your answers in my words, allow the poetry
to heal you.
Words are healing, poetry is healing, even the
kind of poems that seem dark.
Sometimes reading something that highlights
what we are going through is the best kind of
medicine, a reminder that we are not going
through it alone and that in itself can be
life changing.

Stay amazing!

The poems.

'I Want You'

I want moments.
I want to feel everything and not know
what to do with the afterburn, not because
I am lost, I'm not.
I am as far from lost as I can possibly be.
I know what I want; I want you.
I want something real even if it forces me to
stop and question everything I have known to be
true, everything that falls short in comparison
to you because you are my everything and I want
to feel everything even if it hurts me, even if
feeling everything costs me everything, I still
want to feel it all.
And though people will try and convince me that
what I feel isn't real, that I'm somehow confused,
that I don't know my own mind, I promise you that
I will never give in.
They are not me.
They do not understand my heart.
They do not feel the pain in the way I do, knowing
that I cannot hold you and have you look into my
eyes with so much intensity that I need never look
at another again because I will always have you.
These are the moments I want, even if it costs me
everything, even if I have to wait an eternity.
I will always choose you, every single time.
I know what I want; I want you.

- James McInerney.

PASSING
CARS

'Passing Cars'

Passing cars don't hold my gaze, for I
am lost behind these tears.
I sit as still as you now lay; not a
soul could know of the loss I feel.
And yet I notice the journeys length,
the sky above me a perfect blue, there
exists hope in varied shades and hues
but I do not look, they are not you.
Instead, I focus on my every breath,
unsure of where the road may lead,
knowing I could fade without the love
we shared, shall become the silence
in which I'll live as I quietly
grieve.

- James McInerney.

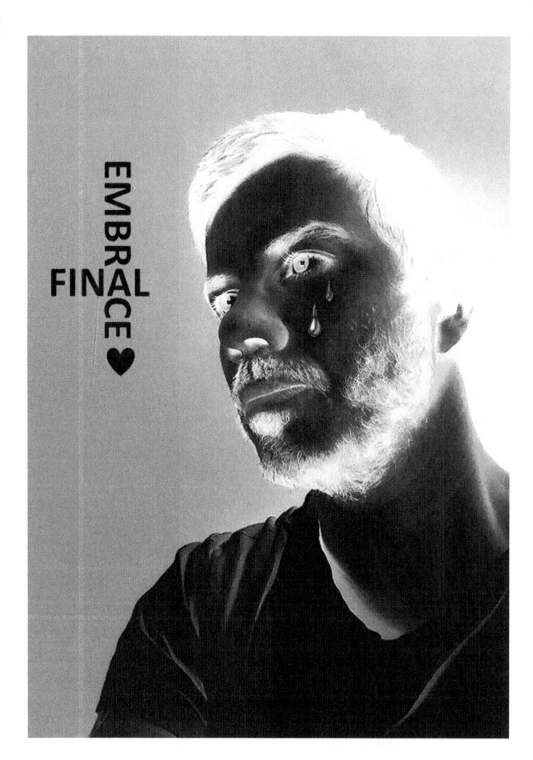

EMBRACE
FINAL ♥

'Final Embrace'

In our final embrace,
let there be enough tears
to stain the world so that
the love we shared shall
never be forgotten.

- James McInerney.

WHEN
I LEAVE

'When I Leave'

When I leave, it will not be to the sound
of synchronised footsteps as I am carried
through a storm of tears; my final memories
won't be of loved ones, all dressed in black,
allowing the bitter aftertaste of sorrow
into their hearts.
No, when I leave it shall be a joyous
occasion, a ticker tape parade, a sea of
every colour - without tide or wave - so
that I may drift at my leisure towards
a glorious end.
And though the sky shall become my resting
place, I will not wear tired eyes that are
required to sleep, nor shall I wallow in
a valley of despair. Instead, I will
become the sun, the moon and all the
stars, forever shining, a constant
reminder to those who I have loved and
who loved me in return that although
there exists a distance between us,
even at its greatest, we shall never
be apart.

- James McInerney.

'Gone'

I no longer live within moments that now
only exist to create memories without
you - they are empty and broken in the
same way that I am.
So I detach myself, a life destined to be
lived in the past, chasing footsteps
made by ghosts that leave me lost.
Yet I still blindly follow, my journey
as endless as time now feels, knowing
I cannot share it with you.

- James McInerney.

MASTERPIECE

'Masterpiece'

It's as though we are constantly reinventing
ourselves to the point that we become
unrecognisable in the end.
A painted planet filled with lost souls,
stained from head to toe, the ink barely dry
before the canvas is reimagined.
Our endless need to create a masterpiece
in a world where everyone is a critic.

- James McInerney.

BELIEVE IN BETTER

'Believe in better'

When it comes to us, I'm impatient, I want
it all, here and now, me and you.
I want moments that mean something, instead
of clinging onto dreams only to have reality
tear them to pieces.
I'm done with destiny, I've put way too much
faith in fate, willing it to open your eyes
in the same way you've opened mine.
Time is precious, we are the higher power,
without the need for intervention or help
that moves at its own pace, drip-feeding
all the hungry souls that are left
unfulfilled.
And I know you're scared, so am I, but it
wouldn't be real love if being real about
how you feel, didn't make your heart race.
So, let go and believe in better, believe
in something bigger than destiny.

Believe in now.

Believe in us.

- James McInerney.

'Ripcord'

Love is bigger than all of us and yet
some still fight it, fearful of the
unknown. However, greatness cannot be
achieved without climbing mountains
and there is no greater achievement
than that of a heart fulfilled.
So, climb these dizzy heights,
overcome your fears and dive head first
into the abyss knowing that when you
pull that ripcord it's because you
are no longer afraid of the fall.

- James McInerney.

CRY

'Cry'

I no longer cry,
I have no more tears,
you took them
the day you promised
to be mine and in my mind,
I believed you were.

- James McInerney.

EMPTY
VESSEL

'Empty Vessel'

I'm addicted to moments that are all I
have left to remind me of you.
I allow them to roam my heart freely,
infecting every chamber without fear of
the fallout. It matters not to me that
my life has become an empty vessel,
forever bound to collect all the
forgotten pieces of you as though the
burden could be so easily erased.
However, in the process of saving you,
I have convinced myself that I am also
being saved too and yet I have never
felt so lost.
I now no longer notice the beauty of
the sky in the same way I used to or
how effortlessly the sun rises and sets
to signal the beginning and end of each
day. For me, there are no days, in the
same way that there are no nights that
remain in which I do not dream of ghosts;
my sleep haunted by visions of you,
of how we were, that stay with me
long after I wake.

- James McInerney.

HOME

'Home'

My home is not made of brick or stone,
it has no walls where pictures hang;
there is no roof sat upon its beams,
to block the sky, I move beneath.
There are no windows to close and lock,
to hide my world behind the glass, it
needs no lights to illuminate even the
darkest of days - it has the sun, the
moon and stars.
There is no number upon its door or a
street in which it will always reside;
my home is not made of brick or stone,
it is wherever you are - you are my
home.

- James McInerney.

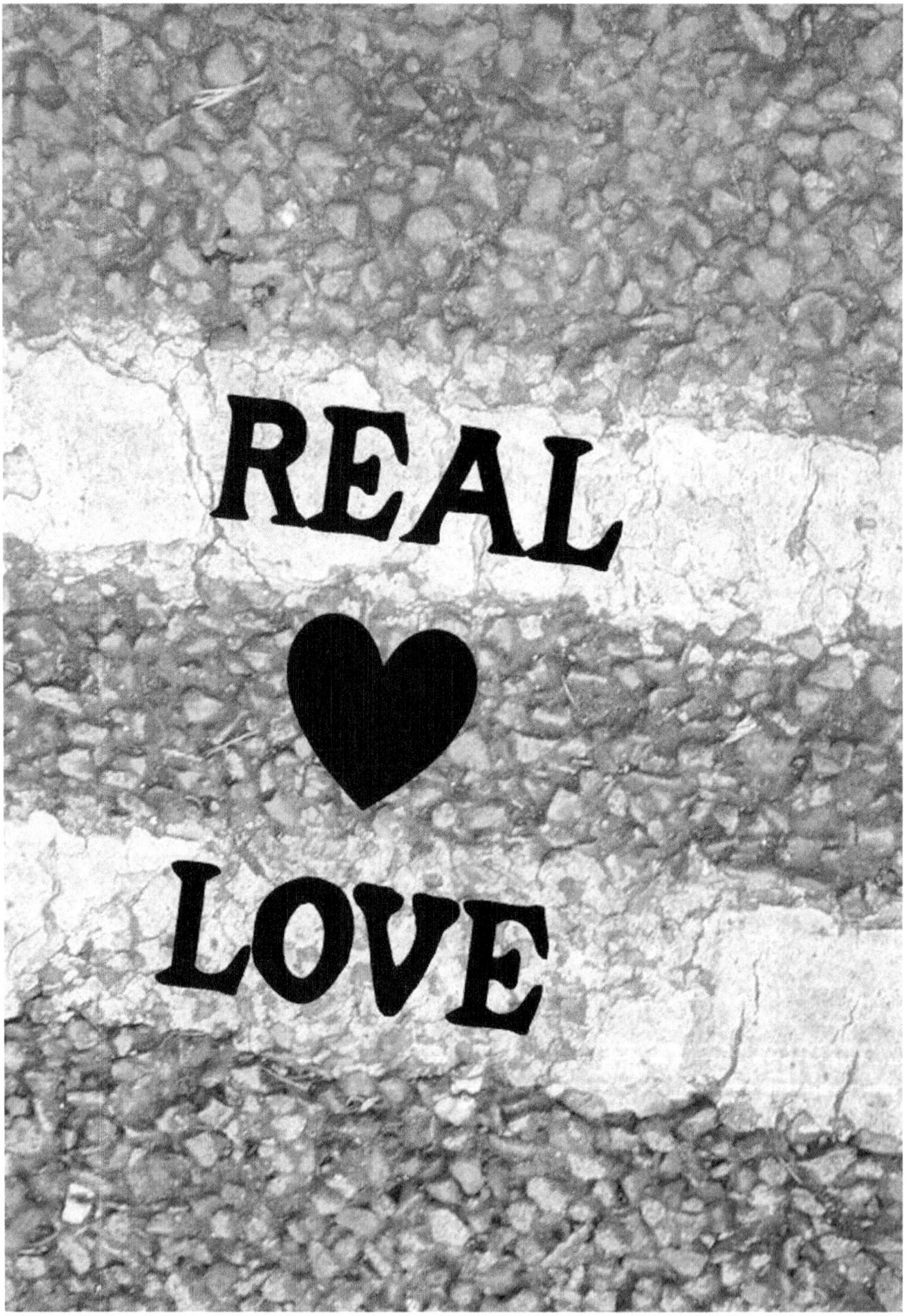
REAL
♥
LOVE

'Real Love'

I know you're scared,
so am I,
but it wouldn't be
real love if being
real about how you
feel, didn't make
your heart race.

- James McInerney.

I AM FIRE

'I am fire'

Go ahead, set fire to all the fields in
which I roam, there will be no flames,
you won't see me burn.
For I am fire and you are not, I've
already made peace with all my demons
regardless of the cost.
There is no storm that runs as wild as
me or a sky as vast or sea as deep.
I breathe in all your fumes and yet
when I exhale, no part of me is lost
at all; for I am fire and you are not,
my flames burn brighter - raw and hot.
The only thing that sets our worlds
apart, is I have nothing left to fear,
not even death can replace the love it
stole from my heart.

- James McInerney.

GLASS

'Glass'

The highways and byways on which I roam
are not covered in gold as once foretold,
nor does there exist, beneath my feet,
diamonds of great fortune that I shall
reap.
The road ahead is littered with glass,
yet it still shines as though inviting
regardless of the splinters and shards.
I brave the journey, my eyes alert,
amongst the chaos and the calm, I traverse.
There are no obstacles that life can
place upon my path or temptations to
blind me and leave behind scars - I am
fearless, forever gaining ground, I push
forward without caution, homeward
bound.

- James McInerney.

SHE OFTEN DREAMS

'She often dreams'

She often dreams
of waking up,
wearing the perfect smile,
but in her heart,
she knows,
without him,
her eyes will always
be opened by tears.

- James McInerney.

THE
POWER

OF
THE
SKY

'The Power of the Sky'

Maybe I allow myself to become distracted
by the daily grind because it's easier
than having to think about you and suffer
the after effects of a broken heart,
every single time.
Nobody should ever have to go through all
that pain and still be expected to find
beauty amongst a night sky, it's impossible
and yet people still do, they are drawn to
it even at the time of their undoing.
They look to the skies in search of that
one star that shines that little bit
brighter than all the others.
It gives them hope, they see themselves,
what they once were and what they will
become again and in that moment, somehow,
the pieces don't seem so broken after
all.

- James McInerney.

THE
RIGHT
KIND
OF
BALANCE

'The Right Kind of Balance'

Loving you gave me wings that allowed me
to fly higher than any cloud, regardless
of the dizzy heights that I reached
whilst in your presence.
My sky became your sky and in our own
way, we worshipped each other like the
lonely souls worship the moon or the
flowers worship the sun.

We were inseparable.

Untouchable.

Existing far beyond the reach of those
that would seek to bring us back down
to earth; we found our own kind of
balance, we overcame the turbulence
and that within itself was its own
kind of beautiful.

- James McInerney.

'She'

She wasn't an adventure,
she was the whole journey.
A beautiful path,
lined with flowers,
that only those who inspired
her heart,were worthy of
walking upon.

- James McInerney.

'Change'

Situations don't change people;
people change people.
You think you know someone and then you
don't; you think you are in love and then
suddenly you're not.
It's as though you thought too much and
ended up giving way too much of yourself
to someone that changed overnight.
One minute you are making lifelong plans,
then in the next breath you're making
different kinds of plans: exit plans,
escape plans, damage limitation plans.
It's no wonder we are all equally as lost;
we are either running from one situation
to the next or running scared - blind to
the dangers.
No one stands still anymore; change isn't
always good. We seem to have forgotten
how to appreciate the moments that matter
most as though they no longer matter
anymore and all we end up with are
situations created by people that end up
changing people forever.

- James McInerney.

EQUAL
MEASURES

'Equal Measures'

I will not be the flame that fuels your
fire until all my energy is spent and
you move onto another.
My heart is complex, it has many chambers
but within each chamber, I am my own
fire - a living, breathing, self-fulfilling
force, strong enough to withstand even the
loneliest of hearts that often come disguised
as love.
You will not drain me of my worth, I am worth
more than that and always will be.
If we are to share the same love, it must be
in equal measures or simply not at all.

- James McInerney.

'Wild Flower'

She would always compare herself to
that of a wild flower - she flourished
in places where other flowers perished.
Her roots grew deep and fast to ensure
her survival in a world that only
measured beauty as though beauty were
a rose.

- James McInerney.

STATIC

'Static'

When his eyes finally settled upon hers
for the last time, it was as though
every single song he had ever loved,
that had ever meant anything to him,
played all at once and with so much
intensity that their parting words
became lost amongst the sound.
As he reached out his hand, in the
hope she would do the same and they
would meet somewhere in the middle,
far from the chaos, all he felt was
how empty and lonely love can be
when it's not reciprocated and instead
of holding onto the hope that kept
him balanced, he gave himself to the
overwhelming tones of sorrow and sadness
that clung to his clothes like static -
tiny electrical charges that could
never restart his broken heart.

- James McInerney.

MOMENTS

'Moments'

Every day I feel you leave me more and
more and yet I still stay; I endure
what I cannot control because you are
all I have left.
Without you, I am all the moments I
swore I would never become and yet,
somehow, as the days pass, I am stood
still, surrounded by a world I once
created so that I could fill it with
you, only to find it empty.

- James McInerney.

'You'

You are the reason my heart keeps
on beating; this world is impossible
but you make it possible for me
to breathe so that I can be me again,
so that I can love you with all that
I am in the hope you will love me
back.

- James McInerney.

SUNSHINE AND RAIN

'Sunshine and Rain'

It's amazing how a single day of sunshine
can erase a lifetime of rain, everything
is somehow temporarily forgotten.
Don't get me wrong, it's not as though I
don't welcome the rain, I do.
It makes me stronger, its waters nourish
my roots and I grow as a person.
I appreciate and accept that there will be
days that the sky will fall and I will be
at its mercy but there is something beautiful
about that - being powerless when the moment
requires it can also be empowering too.
However, sometimes, we all need warmth in our
life, it allows our bones the time they
need to recover so they don't feel so heavy.
Too much heavy isn't good for the soul.
The soul was born to fly, it can never
truly be free if the weight of the world
is always upon it.
So, if we are to thrive, the chemistry
must be right, our bodies need everything
in equal measures:
sunshine and rain,
love and loss,
joy and fear,
a beginning and an end,
and of course, you and me.

- James McInerney.

A HEART
FULL
OF
LOVE

'A Heart Full of Love'

As she lay in his arms, her words were few
but they carried so much weight.

"Will you still love me tomorrow?"

His response was immediate without pause
or hesitation.

"No."

"I will love you with all that I am today,
 tomorrow can wait its turn."

She found herself smiling regardless of
the tiredness that hung heavy upon her bones.
Sleep would not win here,
her heart was full,
full of love.

- James McInerney.

BEAUTIFUL

'Beautiful'

There is nothing more
beautiful than slowing
down and appreciating
the moment with the
upmost respect it so
rightly deserves.

- James McInerney.

STRAIGHT LINES

'Straight Lines'

We all move forward in one direction;
however, sometimes, even straight lines
have curves.
The difference can be subtle, unnoticed
but over time that brief exhale can turn
into an uncontrollable need to breathe
as though the world lacked enough air.
If there were straight lines then maybe
love would be easier to deal with;
the road ahead would be smoother and
there would be no need for our hearts
to rest within their cage, fearful of
the dangers but they do.
We are prisoners within our own bodies,
not so much 'soul mates' more like
'cell mates', hidden from sight.
Be that as it may, those that dare,
the kind of people who wear their
heart on their sleeve, maybe they
are the curves, subtle and unnoticed,
a distraction from the righteous road
and it's not until we collide with them,
until we fall blindly in love, allowing
the two paths to align that the damage
is already done and the straight lines
are no longer straight lines anymore.

- James McInerney.

BRIDGES

'Bridges'

True love shouldn't be hidden,
it should be celebrated and
welcomed as though it were
absolutely everything.
Real love, the kind that lasts,
is the coming together of
two souls lit by the same
flame, a unity that goes beyond
words and yet words are so
important - they build bridges
that conquer land and sea,
they offer hope to the broken
hearted, they defy distance,
a distance that always keeps
you hidden from me.

- James McInerney.

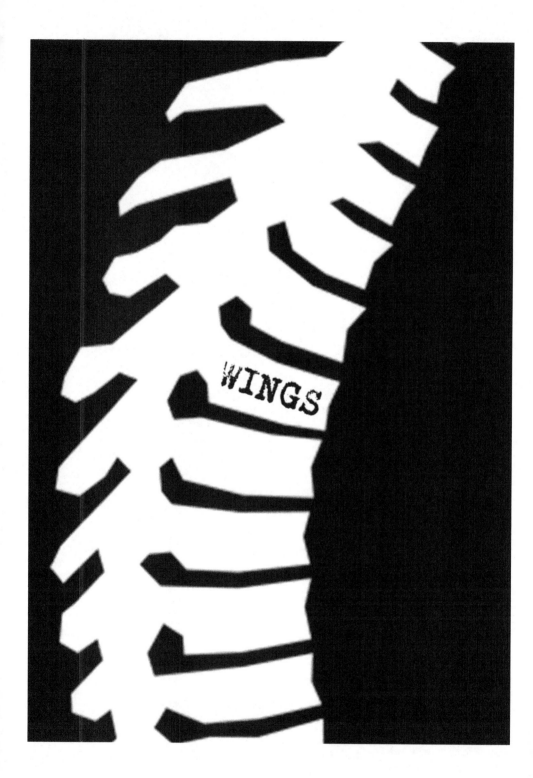

'Wings'

I need never fly,
it keeps me from you.
I want to break
these wings
and have the pieces
bury deep
into the depths
of your back,
along the length
of your spine
so that you feel
me beneath your
skin, every time
you breathe.

- James McInerney.

Oxygen

8

O

15.999

'Oxygen'

I can't promise you all of me, not all of
the time. Even something as complex and
ferocious as fire still needs oxygen in
order to survive otherwise it suffocates
and dies.
If you are to love me, you must allow me
the freedom to be able to spread my wings
and fly so that I can feel comfortable
in my own skin or I will always feel
trapped and my heart will be of no use
to anyone.
I am not something to be kept; kept things
end up gathering dust and it slowly
consumes them until they are unable to
breathe.
I can't burn bright if I cannot breathe,
in the same way that I cannot love you
with all that I am if you want all of
me, all the time.

- James McInerney.

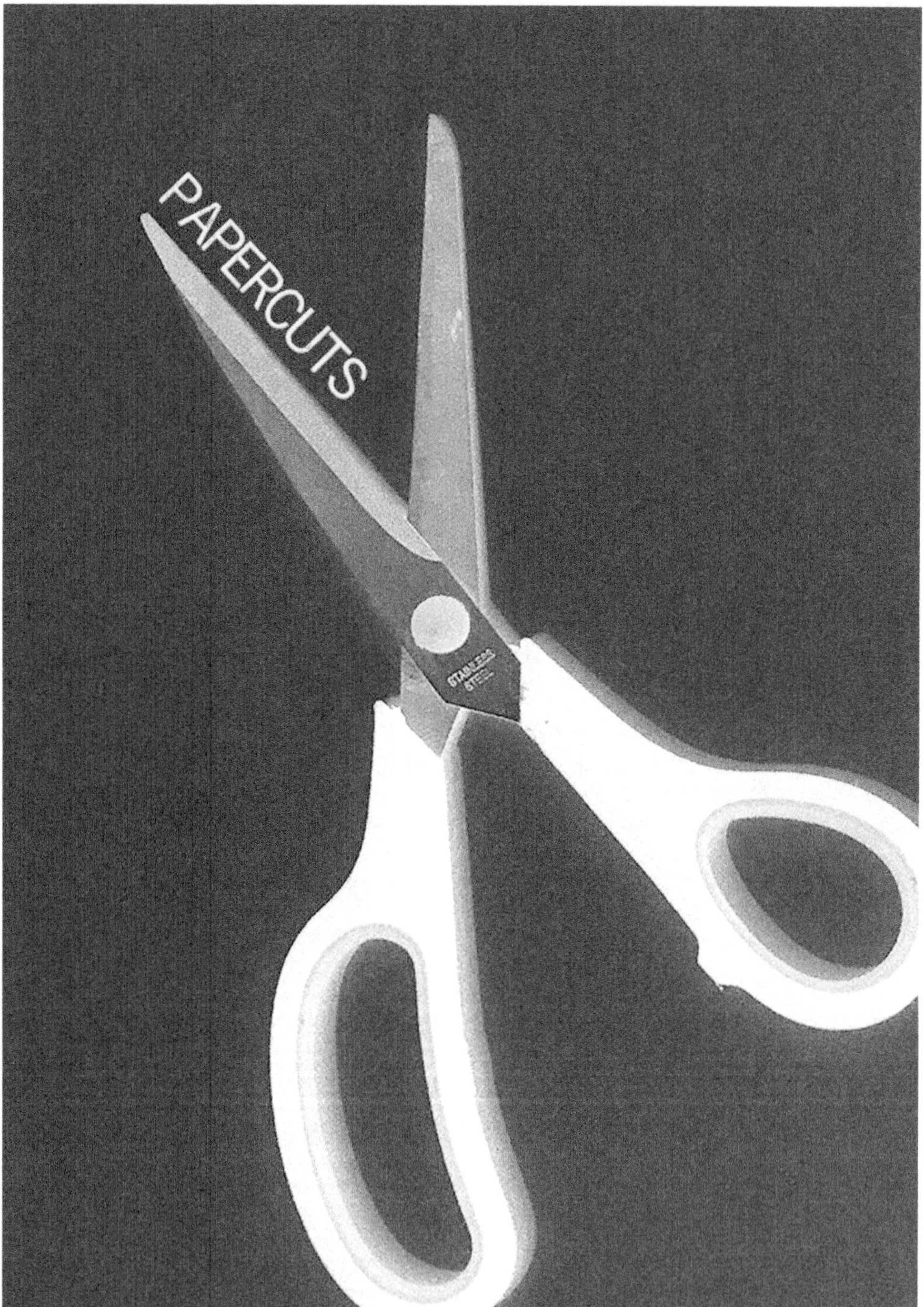
PAPERCUTS
STAINLESS STEEL

'Papercuts'

The ink is barely dry and yet the final
words are said; silence lingers at the
edges - its pain, sharp and tender to
the touch.
Every rewrite, every edit, matters not
for all is lost; time is stolen as though
unworthy, regardless of the cost.
Empty pages, empty spaces, papercuts that
create scars; never more, never less,
forever present in our hearts.

- James McInerney.

LOVE
LOVE
LOVE
LOVE

'Tragic Things'

Sometimes
in
life,
tragic
things
often
come
disguised
as
love.

- James McInerney.

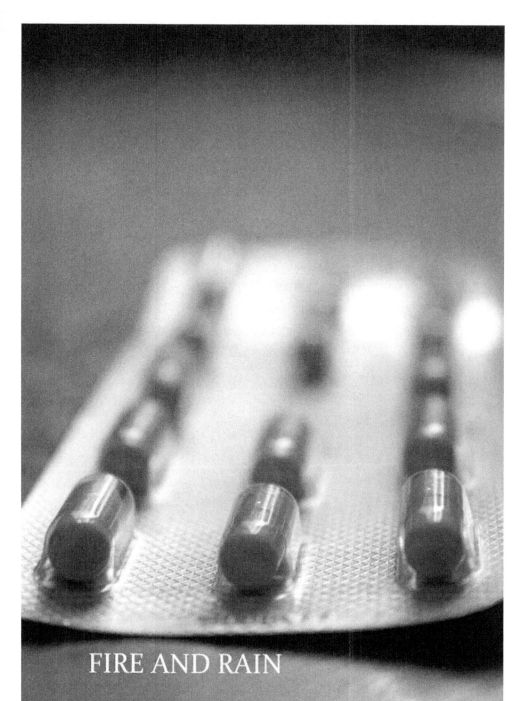

FIRE AND RAIN

'Fire and Rain'

I often wonder how the world managed to
break you, how much rain it took to put
out your fire.
Nothing shone brighter, not even the glory
of a perfect sunrise could compare - you
were beyond beautiful, you were my 'beautiful'.
I can only imagine the pain you felt, how
you would have fought with all that you
were until the very end, heartbroken that
it still wasn't enough, yet you still
fought.
I admire your courage, the bitter pill is
hard to swallow, especially when you are
being force fed false hope just to satisfy
the needs and hunger of others.
I wish I could have been there, we could
have saved each other, taking our broken
pieces and aligning them in such a way
that the cracks remain hidden from view,
in the way that I am now hidden from the
world without you - constantly looking
to the skies waiting for it to rain so
that I can be with you once again.

- James McInerney.

'Flowers'

The flowers did not die in vain,
they were admired for their beauty
as though it was all they had to
offer.
Their petals fell and faded where
they lay - unnoticed and rotten -
it mattered not to the world of
the struggle they'd endured as they
returned to the soil from where
they once came, so something
beautiful could grow in their
place and be forgotten all the same.

- James McInerney.

'All the Things'

I want to feel all the things
you've never felt and give
them to you in such a way that
it shocks you to your very
core and opens your eyes to a
world in which I promised to
never let go of you.

- James McInerney.

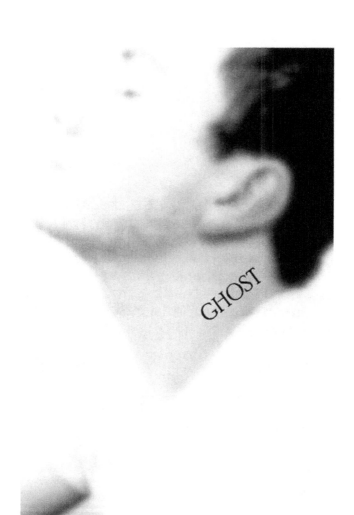

'Ghost'

Death isn't what breaks the heart and soul
of those that are left behind, it's an
inevitable means to an end, as is the night
sky that draws each day to a close.
However, being alone for what seems like an
eternity without the one person you promised
forever to, goes far beyond the realms of
death or pain.
It matters not how or when the day ends for
it has no meaning when it's spent alone.
To have you stood before me, knowing I can
no longer be yours is unbearable.
I see the tears that you hide as you're
brought down to your knees, hoping and
praying that something more than silence
will catch your fall but it never does.
How I wish I could be the one to comfort
you, our bodies intertwined with so much
unity that there exists no higher power
strong enough to tear us apart, and yet we
remain apart. Isolated. Entities that were
once breathing the same air, feeling the

same things, loving without measure,
and because of our love, I can't help but
feel the weight of the world as though I
still belong, even if it means I will always
be nothing more than a ghost to you.

- James McInerney.

COLD BONES

'Cold Bones'

All the coldness in this world, takes its
toll on my bones; I cannot move without
feeling lost and yet I'm forced to feel
everything alone.
I see bodies everywhere, above me and below,
they move in circles as though uncertain
of the life they used to own.
No sun have I at all, only clouds that
cover my sky; you were once the fire that
warmed my soul but the flames burned too
bright and life stole your light, now all
I feel is the coldness in this world
as it takes its toll on my bones.

- James McInerney.

THE GIRL
IN THE
MIRROR

'The girl in the mirror'

A girl sits alone, her only comfort,
a mirror.
It smiles at her fondly, without pause
or hesitation.
Although its face looks like hers,
somehow, they are completely different -
she doesn't feel the same inside,
regardless of the reflection.
Every cut,
every scar,
still as raw as can be,
no longer hidden from the world and yet
the world will always see, the girl in
the mirror, her smile, not the tears.

- James McInerney.

ALL
THE
LIGHTS

'All the Lights'

Of all the lights
that shine, you
will always be
the most beautiful
star, sat amongst
the night sky,
that my eyes settle
upon.

- James McInerney.

A LIGHT THAT BURNS BRIGHT

'A light that burns bright'

And so, we stand, lost amongst the
inequalities that scar our skin on a
daily basis, forcing us to bleed.
We shed tears when life lets us down and
yet carries on regardless.
We reach out, across the darkened divide,
knowing that sometimes, nothing or no one
will hold our hand but we still reach,
awash with hope and nothing more.
And in our time of need, in our hour of
darkness, it is our overwhelming belief
in faith, in the greater good, that keeps
us strong.
And though there are those of us that
don't believe, when the moment arrives
and our test is true, the light inside
that went away, somehow manages to burn
brighter than ever before.

- James McInerney.

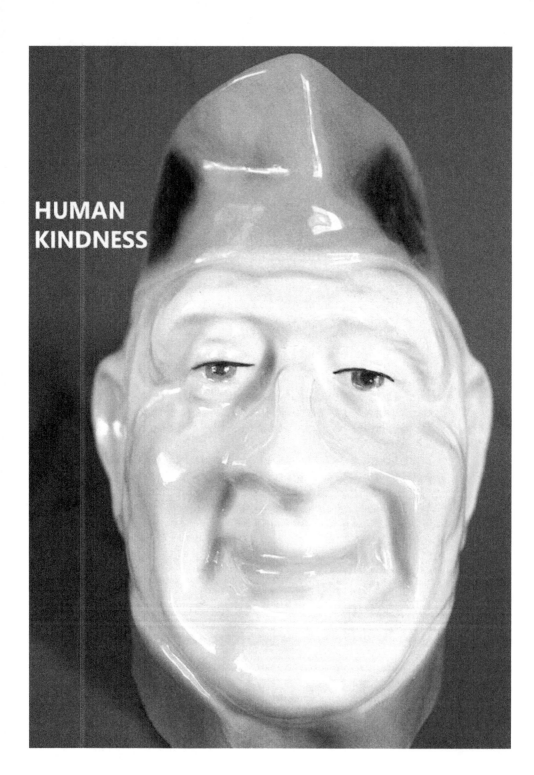

HUMAN
KINDNESS

'Human Kindness'

I love moments of human kindness.
Like a besotted observer, I can't help
but watch as two strangers, who shall
probably never meet again, pause to
acknowledge each other and take a
much-needed time out from their chaotic
lives to smile and say "hello".
Somehow in that split second the world
is a better place.
And as I watch from a distance, I find
myself lost in the moment, wishing
that could have been me.

- James McInerney.

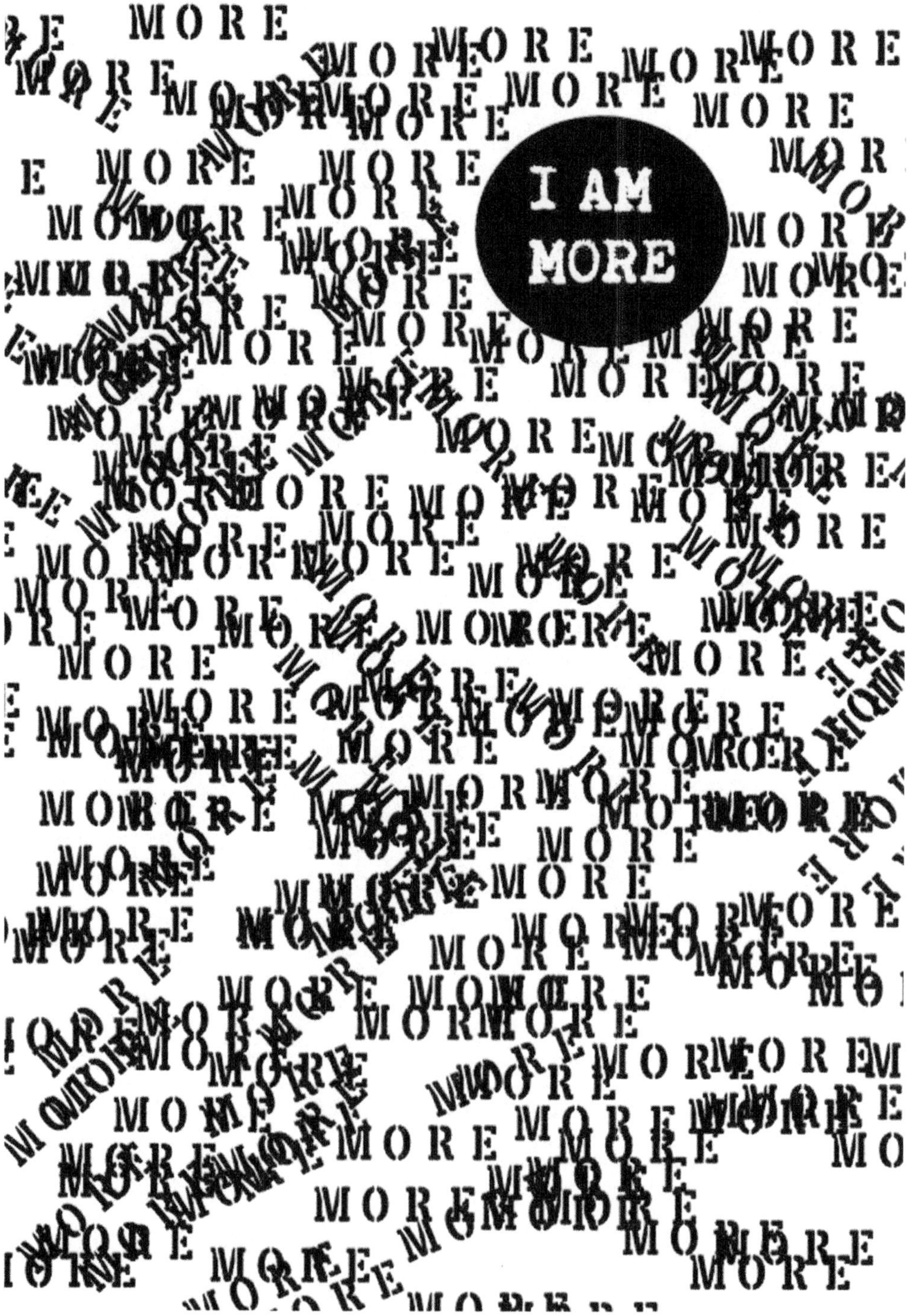
I AM MORE

'I am more'

I am more
than you will
ever need and
yet you always
seem to have
a constant
need for
something
more than
me.

- James McInerney.

'Same Sky'

I often dream of us as though we are still
part of the same sky, two stars that
shone so bright, even the sun became
envious of the 'love light' we emitted.
We were our own universe, a force so
undeniable that there existed no
gravitational pull strong enough to
keep us apart and yet somehow, we drifted.
We became lost.
Untangled.
Separated by galaxies and a distance
that defined our borders.
The walls were built so high, it was as
though we no longer belonged.
However, in spite of the pain, I still
shone for you. I still willingly gave
myself to the moon each night and worshipped
it without question, in the hope that
you were doing the same too because there
is no moon without the stars in the same
way that there is no me without you.

- James McInerney.

LET
IT
BE

'Let it be'

If we are to collide, let it be together
and with so much force that even death
itself won't be able to tear us apart.
Let us jump willingly into the abyss,
unafraid of the fall, knowing that we
were not pushed, instead our bodies
simply let go of all the things they
used to cling to that weighed them
down.

- James McInerney.

'You and I'

Look at all the dreamers,
dreaming in the sky,
their bodies dancing without worry,
far beyond the clouds upon high.
That was us once,
you and I,
now all we do is watch them from
a distance,
wearing wings that weigh us down,
that neither soar or fly.

- James McInerney.

AS HE
STOOD
BEFORE
HER

'As he stood before her'

As he stood before her, one last time,
she could hear the sound of her heart breaking
and yet she fought back the tears.
She wanted so desperately to reach out and touch
the glass, to have her hand match the shape of
his as though they were meant to be, regardless
of the pain it caused her.
She wanted to tell him everything.
She wanted to let him know how much he had hurt
her and yet regardless of that, how much she still
loved him.
But she couldn't.
The words refused to form in her mouth and in an
instant, he was gone and she knew the darkness
that clouded her vision, that made the world
seem that little bit smaller, would hurt her
more than he ever could.

- James McInerney.

MY BIGGEST MISTAKE

'My Biggest Mistake'

My biggest mistake was believing I could
seek out beauty in even the darkest of
places and give it wings to set it free
in the hope it would somehow love me
but it never did.
In my search, I became lost and without
realising it, the coldness slowly crept
into my bones and I foolishly embraced
it as though it was all I deserved,
unaware that I deserved so much more.

- James McInerney.

'I Love You'

I love you
without
question
and yet I
always find
myself
questioning
the love you
have for me.

- James McInerney.

"Target Practice'

Do not tell me you love me unless you have
learnt to love youself first; my heart isn't
target practice for people with itchy trigger
fingers who cannot aim straight.
If you shoot and miss, I will be left with the
bullet holes, wounds that take an eternity to
heal.
I cannot allow that.
I will not be cannon fodder just because you
found a loaded gun and got caught up in the
moment without truly knowing how to use it
properly.
It is important that you are comfortable in
your own skin before I allow you the freedom
to roam beneath mine, otherwise you will
never truly appreciate how much damage three
simple words can do when you don't fully
understand their impact.
So, do not tell me you love me, until you
have truly learnt to love yourself first.

- James McInerney.

'Taller than trees'

My love for you has roots that run
deeper than those on even the tallest
of trees. It is adventureus and wild,
an uphill pursuit, beckoning me
forever onwards - branch by branch -
regardless of foothold.
I do not fear the unknown, as overwhelming
as it may seem, instead I embrace it;
climbing to heights far beyond my realms
of comfort, knowing if I am ever to be
truly found by you, first I must allow
myself to become lost in the presence
of love.

- James McInerney.

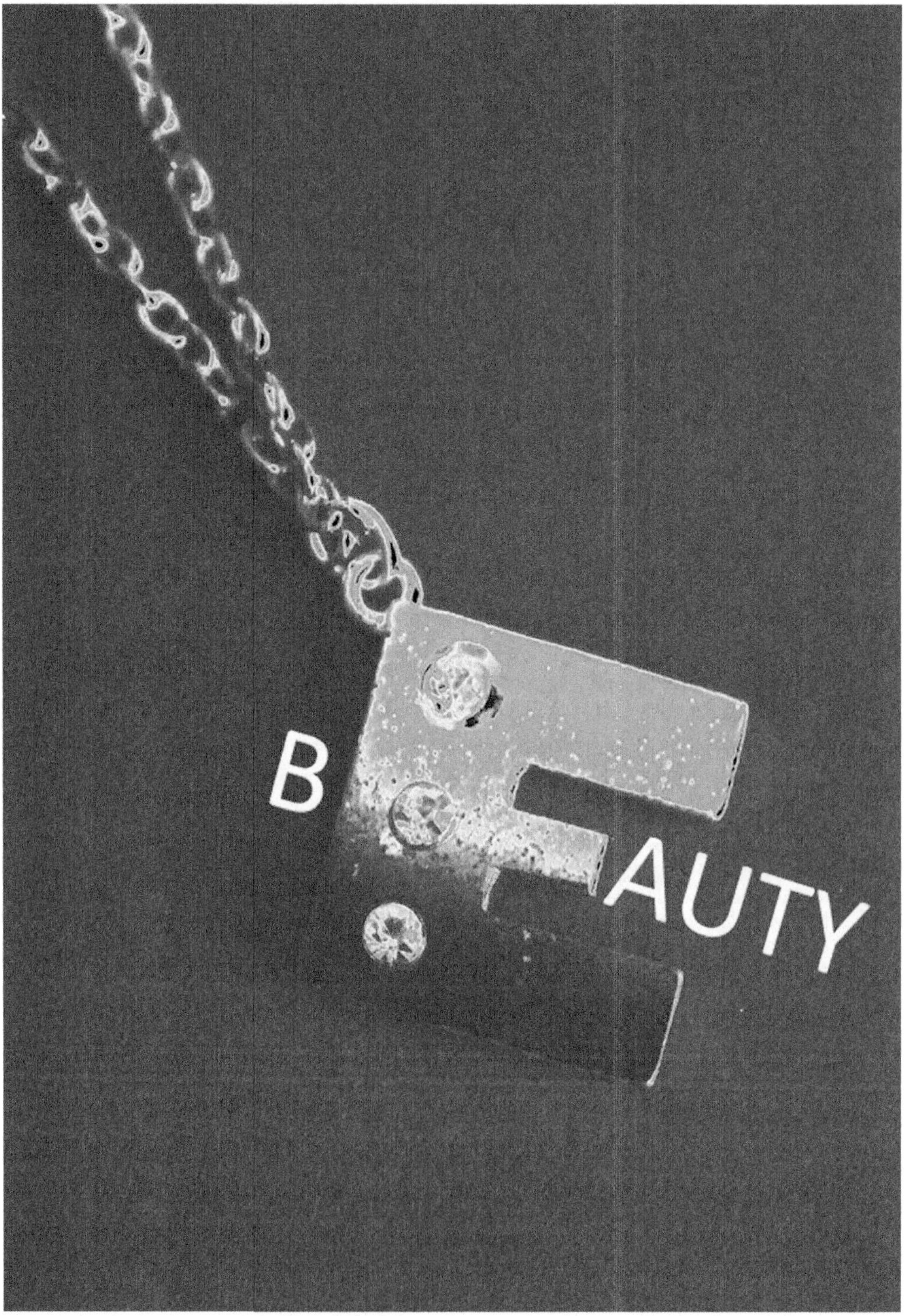
B
AUTY

'Beauty'

If I were to compare you to anything,
it wouldn't be a summers day or the
moon and stars - they already know the
power that their beauty has upon the
hearts of those who gaze upon them so.
You however, have no idea how truly
beautiful you are, nothing can compare
to that.

- James McInerney.

'Storm Chaser'

All I know is this: things become fragile
and unstable when pressure is applied
to their surface, however, I would walk
without fear, across a sea of glass if it
meant I could be with you.
You are at the epicentre of every storm
I have ever chased and will always chase,
regardless of the fallout.
Even at their greatest, nobody ever comes
close. There will never be anyone who
will mean as much to me as you do right
now and yet we exist forever at a distance
as though the world deems us unworthy of
breathing the same air but we are so
worthy, so goddamn worthy that it hurts
to breathe alone, without you.

- James McInerney.

COLLIDE

'Collide'

Maybe we are all equally lost and in
the confusion, as we collide, somehow
the pieces manage to fall and fit in
the way they are supposed to.
Take love for example, to truly reach
its dizzy heights, you have to dive
headfirst into the abyss, unprepared
for the collision, guided only by a
reckless heart and an open mind.

- James McInerney.

SUNSHINE

'Sunshine'

My life
without your love,
is like
feeling the warmth
of a perfect summer
sunshine,
knowing the curtains
will forever
remain closed.

- James McInerney.

'Music'

I would dance with you but my heart won't
allow it, regardless of the desire I can
no longer contain.
I find myself constantly having to fight
the urge to let go in such a way that
it mirrors your every move.
You are the music, an entire orchestra -
pitch perfect - that requires no rehearsal
at all.
So, I listen, my eyes closed.
It matters not to me that 'others' admire
your beauty; they cannot hear what I hear,
feel the way I feel or know of the pain I
endure every time I have to watch you dance
alone, without me.

- James McInerney.

FOREVER LOVE

'Forever Love'

I still dream of you and yet my eyes
refuse to close, your sky above me dark,
its hands around my throat.
I count each and every breath as though
it were my last, focused on all the
empty spaces that sit heavy upon my
broken heart.
No tears have I that break, not a single
one; time holds me close and I am
frozen, forced to endure the love we
once shared . . . . alone.

- James McInerney.

AVENUES AND ALLEYWAYS

'Avenues and Alleyways'

My love for you
consists of
avenues
and
alleyways,
dreams in which I
often spend my
days alone,
in search of you.

- James McInerney.

ANGELS
AND
MONSTERS

'Angels and Monsters'

At the time of my undoing, I built an army
without knowing, to fight the demons
you left behind.
Comprised of angels and monsters,
caught between love and betrayal,
there waged a war in the corners of my mind.
I saw darkness and destruction,
old wounds opened, once hidden,
that woke a fire in me, beyond all control.
Every nightmare a vision, a series of
delayed premonitions, bearing the illusion
of loves welcoming smile.
As my rage grew and grew, fuelled by memories
of you, I surrendered every piece of myself
to the cause.
Unaware as I did, how all my angels hid,
fearful of the monster I had become inside.

- James McInerney.

ALONE

'Alone'

Oh, what I would give to have you
look at me in the way I look at you,
knowing I need never fear the
trappings of rejection.
What a feeling that would be.
I would live within the moment for
an eternity - overjoyed and breathless.
Nothing else would matter, not even
the moments I have endured without
you where I felt isolated from
everyone and everything around me,
wanting someone to notice me,
always hoping it would be you,
only to find myself forever alone.

- James McInerney.

I AM IN LOVE WITH THE SEA

'I am in love with the sea'

I am in love with sea.
Even though it's wild, ferocious and
unpredictable, it still calms me like
no other ever could and yet its waves
that always greet me, offering hope
when hope is lost, always break,
only to be dragged back out by the
tide far from the reach of my shore.

- James McInerney.

WRITING
TO
REMEMBER

'Writing to Remember'

If there should ever come a day that I
no longer find pieces of you buried
deep within my words, then I will
stop and allow the ink to dry for
the final time.
If I am to write, it will not be about
'ghosts'; you are very much alive.
A living, breathing, heartbeat that I
spend all my time reading over and over
just so I can hear the sound of your
voice in my head and have it feel as
though you never left me in the most
tragic of ways.

- James McInerney.

I

AM

MY

OWN

ISLAND

'I am my own island'

I am my own island
regardless of the sea
that slowly devours me
at my shore.

My heart is kept at
the heart of me,
a hidden treasure,
buried deep.

The raging tides
that ebb and flow
neither push or pull
me from where I stand;
I am my own island,
I am me,
regardless of the tide or sea.

- James McInerney.

'Hide and Seek'

Forgotten things eventually fade,
like the love we once shared.
A place in which I would often hide,
hoping you would seek me out,
only to find myself alone -
forever lost.

- James McInerney.

THE
LONGEST
PAUSE

'The Longest Pause'

The longest pause, that's how I am reminded
of you.
I gave you everything, even the parts of
myself that you only give when you are
absolutely sure it's real.
It felt real.
You convinced me.
There weren't the familiar seams to pick at
and feel the ache as they slowly unravelled.
Something my heart had learnt to accept and
yet I now find myself alone.
A shadow amongst the shadows.
Unnoticed.
Forgotten.
As far as a person can possibly be from
themselves before they end up being
someone else.
Someone different.
Someone broken.

- James McInerney.

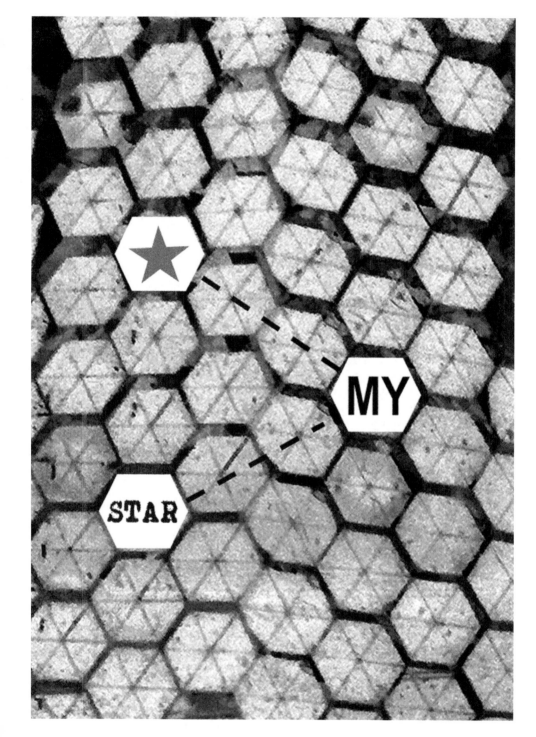

'My Star'

I no longer fear the future,
not because I'm immune to death,
no one is.
The truth is, I found you and you
found me and although that might
not mean much to anyone else,
to me it's life changing.
I awake each morning with a
purpose, a hope renewed.
You gave me that and it was in
that moment that I knew there
were no more galaxies that I
wanted to explore - I had
found my star.

- James McInerney.

'Perfectly Aligned'

In slow motion,
our bodies collide,
we are dancers,
without the music
and yet we always move in rhythm,
two souls bound together
for an eternity,
perfectly aligned.

- James McInerney.

'In every possible moment'

In every possible moment, I'm as much you
as you are me.
Two souls connected as though a single
entity and yet we exist, worlds apart.
The flame in which we find ourselves
burning, only burns because we burn -
our love its fuel, our hope its embers
that eventually fade until all that
remains are ashes and dust.
Remnants that get taken by the wind.
We become lost and in the process, it
changes who we are, who we were and who
we eventually become.

- James McInerney.

BENEATH THE SKY

'Beneath the sky'

Beneath the sky my body floats, without
ears or mast to guide me home; no worries
have I, not a single one, they pass
unheard at depths unknown.
For I am free, my troubles gone, regardless
of the rising tide. I no longer fear the
waves which move me so - I belong to every
ebb and flow.
The sun, the moon, the stars above, I still
see them though my eyes are closed. Without
ears or mast to guide me home, beneath
the sky, my body floats.

- James McInerney.

JACKET

'Jacket'

I've learnt to live with the pain,
to appreciate its flaws,
its vulnerabilities,
its weaknesses because they are the
same as mine.
I wear it well,
as though it were a favourite jacket,
high collar,
snug against my skin,
so I cannot tell where it ends
and I begin.

- James McInerney.

THE RIGHT SIDE OF BAD

'The right side of bad'

When it comes to you, I'm always on the
right side of bad, far from the reach
of every demon that you harbour to
atone for all the devils I lack.
No lines are crossed, not a single one,
within the ever-changing boundaries,
I hide my ever-changing love.
Not a single footstep is misplaced or
words spoken that can't be unsaid,
I burn without your love and yet whilst
in your presence, I am an island of
regret.The surrounding tides speak
only of the sorrow I endure, keeping
you forever at a distance from me,
far beyond the wildest waters that
I'm forbidden to tread.

- James McInerney.

'I Came Back'

I came back,
back to me,
freed from the fortress
that had become my prison,
in which I became lost.
Its darkened walls,
an eternal cross,
upon which my body hung alone.
But my eyes were opened,
the visions blinding,
I saw everything
as though I was seeing it
for the first time.
Things that were always there,
things that I had always seen.
I saw you,
I saw us,
and I came back,
back to me.

- James McInerney.

MY MOON

'My Moon'

Without you, oh how I often find myself
lost; my broken heart comparable to that
of a forgotten star, set adrift in a sky
so vast, forever searching for that
reassuring pull of its moon to keep it
perfectly aligned so that it may once
again shine.

- James McInerney.

'Not me, Not I'

My eyes are open, wide open, as is
my heart when it comes to you but I
will not be caught in the crossfire
if we are to collide.
I do not need another bullet buried
deep in my chest, with your name on
it, just to open my eyes to the
dangers of unrequited love.
I am in full control of my own heart;
I follow no one.
I have the strength and patience to
stand my ground and allow the roots
that bind, to take hold until you
are gone.

- James McInerney.

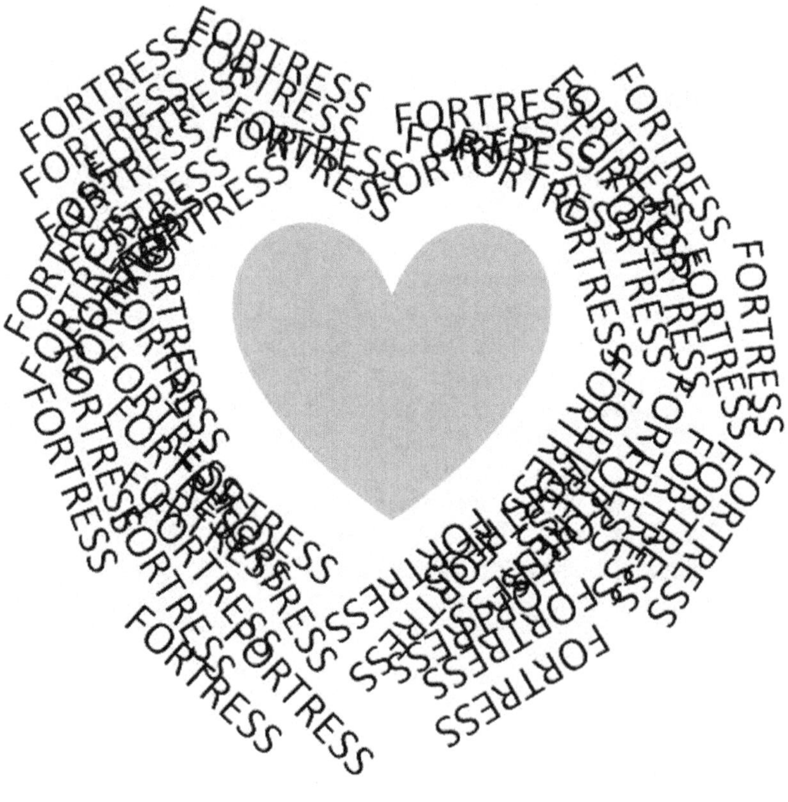

'Fortress'

What was 'freedom' to a girl who could
construct a fortress around herself
in a heartbeat?
A defence mechanism against everything
life had to offer.
She had become used to recognising
the markings of defeat because they were
tattooed all over her arms like war wounds,
tiny precision cuts, hidden away from the
eyes of the world.
For her, it was easier not to believe in
love, when all the things she loved and
thought loved her, quickly faded from
view.

- James McInerney.

'Heavy Heart'

Only take from this life, what you need
to repair the parts of yourself that
love broke.
When we carry things with us on our
journey that have no use other than
to weigh us down, they always sit
heavy upon the heart.

- James McInerney.

'Learning to fly'

If you can find the strength within
yourself to fight back, those glorious
wings of yours, that you never knew you
had, will open and you'll be the master
of the air that once controlled you and
kept you grounded.
The new heights at which you'll soar,
the views that will allow you to observe
the world in its entirety will give you
a much-needed clarity, allowing you to
see the bigger picture so you know what
to change, a change that will start and
end with you.

- James McInerney.

A

FLAME

'A Flame'

The reason you will always find
this life a struggle is because
you are a living, breathing work
of art, who is very much awake
in a world that would rather
you were sedated and docile
because it makes you easier
to handle.
I promise you this, you were
not born to be contained,
that much fire rarely is.
So, rage and burn, even if doing
so makes you wild and uncontrollable.
Become the flame that the darkness
in the world so desperately needs,
a flame that will never die.

- James McInerney.

'Time'

When I am with you,
I do not care about time;
time has a purpose,
regardless of length,
counting down to an end.
Instead I think of a world
without time,
one that is endless,
like my love will always
be for you.

- James McInerney.

'Eternal'

I will follow your path without pause
or regret regardless of the road that
lay ahead.
Each twist and turn comprised of endless
greys, shall be what my heart must
endure until it settles with you.
I will not dwell in empty moments
knowing I do so alone or ponder over
all the memories I long to own,
instead I'll continue to live my life
as though you were here with me.
Forever mine,
forever after,
eternally.

- James McInerney.

AN
ANGEL

'An Angel'

I refuse to believe that you are gone.
In my eyes, you were always an angel,
it just took heaven giving you your wings,
for the world to finally see,
what I've seen all along.

- James McInerney.

'Everywhere I Go'

Everywhere I go, you are with me;
we always spend the days together
even though you are not here.
I've lost count of the time we've
shared because it's eternal,
just like the pain,
the love and the fear.
My eyes still see as though life
were a datdream, my vision plagued
with memories of you; I'd rather go
blind because all I see now are
ghosts stood before me and one of
those ghosts is always you.

-- James McInerney.

'Stones'

The best kind of stones are those
found where the land and the sea
meet, the two forces harmoniously
colliding at the same time and in
the same way, leaving behind
precious memories.
A paradise for all the dreamers
who are drawn to the water's edge
in the hope that they might find
something to have and to hold,
something they can treasure
forever.

- James McInerney.

FLAMES

'Flames'

Remember this:

A fire is still
a fire regardless
of the size of
its flames —
they still burn
and leave
permanent
scars.

- James McInerney.

'Bleeding Heart'

I am a bleeding heart, forced to feel
everything and have it control my thoughts
until they are no longer mine.
Although I walk amongst the wounded, I do
not show them my scars, I hide my pain
behind a well-rehearsed smile in the same
way that they do, knowing in that moment,
in that two second glance as we acknowledge
each other, somehow neither of us are
alone.

- James McInerney.

STARS

'Stars'

Maybe the stars only exist as
a constant reminder to all the
lonely hearts; the pain of
seeing such beauty and having
to love it forever, from a
distance.

- James McInerney.

A
Darkened
Room

'A Darkened Room'

The darkness of the room,
I notice how it sleeps,
subtle and without alarm
and yet a panic inside me speaks.
Fingertips outstretched,
cutting through the air,
the silence fills my ears with sorrow
until it's all I ever hear.
Pictures of us sit,
coated in layers of less,
a plague hangs heavy upon my heart,
immune to death,
in the ways,
you were not.

- James McInerney.

WORK
OF
ART

'Work of Art'

If you are to love me,
it is important you
understand that I am not,
nor will I ever be,
a work of art.
I have flaws,
imperfections,
surface damage - scars
that cannot be erased.
I am not something you
keep hidden away,
behind the confines of
safety glass, afraid I
will deteriorate if
exposed to the same air
in which you freely
roam.

- James McInerney.

I FOUND MYSELF IN YOU

'I Found Myself in You'

I found myself lost
and in the process,
somehow,
my missing pieces
settled within you
as though you were
home, a place I'm
destined to
discover.

- James McInerney.

FINGERTIPS

'Fingertips'

It hurts.

The pain is real.

I feel it.

Your love gave me wings and I foolishly
flew into the sun, attracted to its
warmth, thinking I had found a piece
of sky that was mine.

I'm not myself when I am around you,
I'm someone else, I'm someone new,
something different and yet I feel
old, I grew tired, my bones ache,
my heart aches.

I've tried to let go of you but
I can't, my fingertips cling
onto your hope and it drags me
forever at a distance, far behind
you, until all I am left with is
bloodied knees and wounds that
never heal.

It hurts.

The pain is real.

I feel it.

- James McInerney.

I BECAME
FIRE

'I Became Fire'

I'm not afraid of your fire - I am a fire too.
If I were to fear you - what you are, what
you've become - I would have to fear myself.
I cannot pretend to be something I am not.
I won't!
I have been burnt by love so many times,
the more I became burnt, it became harder
to distinguish myself from that of the
fire, so I became fire.

- James McInerney.

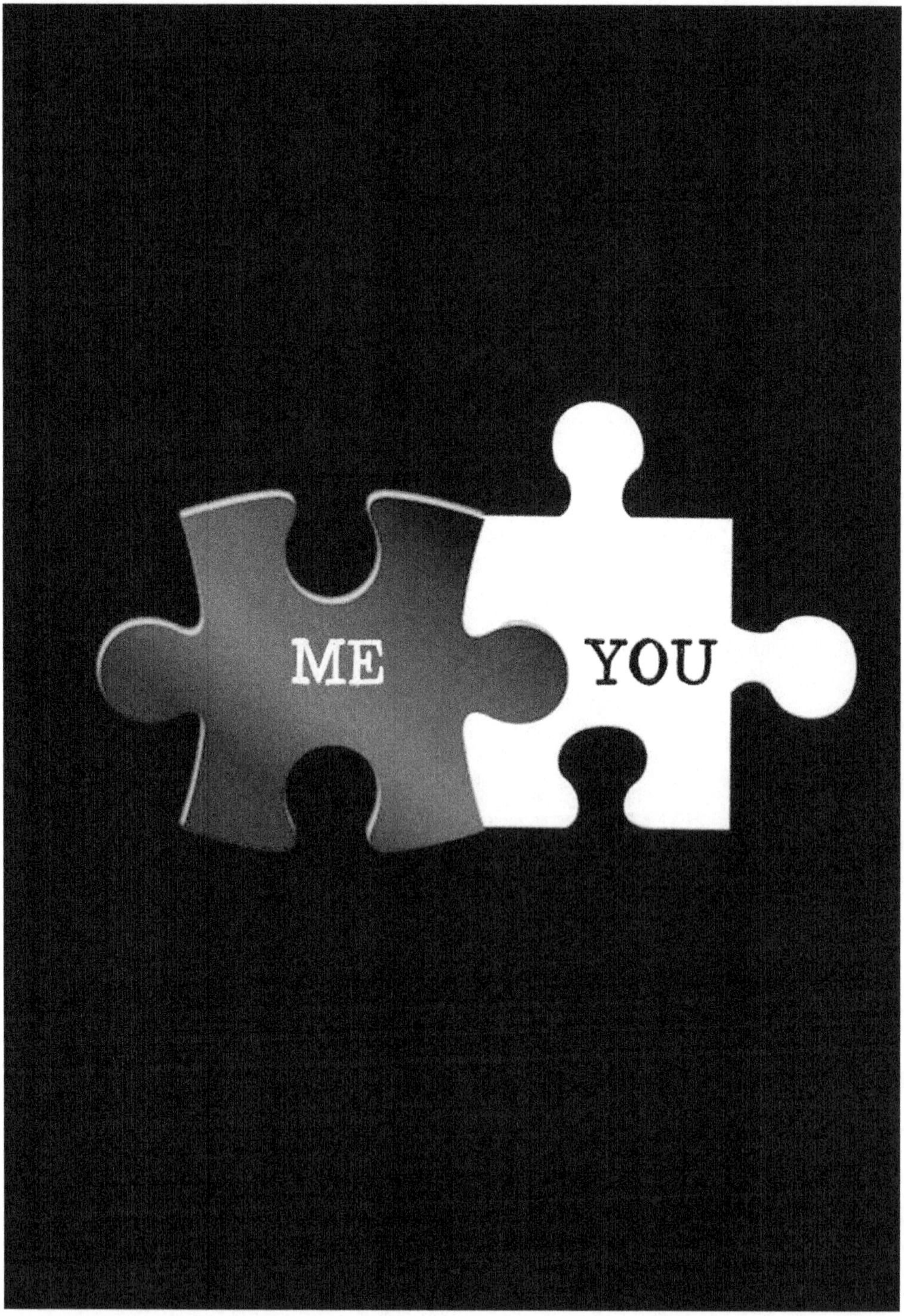
ME
YOU

'Me and You'

Let my body be covered in hands
and those hands always belong to you.
Let them span the length of my spine,
healing every single bruise.
Let us stand in the middle, unharmed,
far from the demons that wreck and
ruin, may our hearts endure it all
and neither falter or break in two
because our strength is stronger
than any fight, our strength is
me and you.

— James McInerney.

Sorrow

'Sorrow'

Sorrow never truly dies, it lives and
breathes in all of us.
Breaking the hearts of even the strongest
of minds, it has no equal in strength
or size.
And yet the fight is often fought, wars
are waged at any cost; in haste, the victors
count their spoils, unaware of what they've
truly lost, for sorrow never truly dies,
it lives and breathes in all of us.

- James McInerney.

WALLS

'Walls'

The love I willingly gave was always
compartmentalised by you as though it was
something to be kept in a box - hidden away.
The perimeters clearly defined.
And yet I still gave, sacrificing the parts
of myself I would never reclaim, without
fully understanding the loss, until I became
lost too.
A wandering soul, searching for the pieces
of my heart that were given without question,
only to be left wanting answers.
I wanted to break down your walls so you could
finally see me but the boundaries ran as deep
as the love I once hoped you had for me.
It's no wonder I felt trapped, my life in
limbo.
But in my moment of weakness, I didn't run or
hide, I embraced my demons and in turn they
smiled back at me in the way you always did
and I foolishly convinced myself you were
still mine.

- James McInerney.

About the Author

James grew up in an area in Northampton aptly
named 'Poets Corner', unbeknownst that poetry
was to become a huge part of his life.
Having no prior interest in the subject matter
in his younger years, James discovered the
wonders of writing in his twenties.
Mixing his own thoughts and emotions with
classical and instrumental film scores, he
realised for the first time in his life that
there was more to writing than met the eye.
With no real influences or coming from a writing
background, James' enthusiasm grew and grew, and
it was full steam ahead - with no turning back!
Not content with writing words for his own
amusement, he continued to test the boundaries -
to great effect.
Using his new-found love for writing and his
in-depth knowledge of social networking sites,
his resourcefulness resulted in success.
As his work is becoming more popular, his numbers
are growing on his social networking sites;
James has over 30,000 followers on Instagram and
over 9,000 followers on Twitter.
Attracting a lot of attention over the years, James
and his works have covered a wide range of different
media platforms.
With his works, he has been featured in various UK
and international magazines and newspapers and has
been featured on various radio stations in the UK
and the Netherlands, including the BBC.
His words have been adapted and performed by many
musicians and vocalists; his first book was also
used in an American Sci-Fi TV show.
With various US/UK actors and actresses voicing
his poetry, James is taking his words to a whole
new level.
His books are currently available to buy via
Amazon Worldwide and are also available to read
for free in various schools, colleges, universities
and libraries in the UK, Ireland and America.

You can keep up to date with James and his
latest works on any of the following sites:

Official Website:
http://jamesmcinerney.wixsite.com/poetry

Facebook:
https://www.facebook.com/borntobeapoet
https://www.facebook.com/groups/JamesTMcInerney/
https://www.facebook.com/jamesmcinerneypoetry/
https://www.facebook.com/groups/thepoetryproject08/

Twitter:
https://twitter.com/millsmc07

Instagram:
https://www.instagram.com/millsmc07

Tumblr:
https://www.tumblr.com/blog/jamesmcinerneyofficial

LinkedIn:
https://www.linkedin.com/in/james-mcinerney-661561128/

Goodreads:
https://www.goodreads.com/author/show/4733780.James_
McInerney

Pinterest:
https://www.pinterest.co.uk/jeetmc07/

Mirakee:
http://www.mirakee.com/jamesmcinerney

YouTube:
http://www.youtube.com/user/millsmc1977

Email:
jeeter77@gmail.com

Google:
Search 'james mcinerney poet'